CW00381224

TANTRIC SEX

Sofia Henndrix

© Copyright 2022 by Sofia Henndrix - All rights reserved.

This document is a useful resource written to provide exact and reliable information regarding the topic covered.

From a Declaration of Principles which was accepted and approved equally by a Committee of the American Bar Association and a Committee of Publishers and Associations. In no way is it legal to duplicate, reproduce, transfer, or transmit any part of the document or content contained therein. All right reserved.

The information contained herein is truthful and consistent with the author's knowledge and is meant for informational purposes only. Hence, any liability accrued from inattention, usage, or abuse of any of the content contained herein is the solitary responsibility of the recipient. The presentation of the information is without contract or guarantee assurance whatsoever.

The author bears no liability whatsoever in relation to the direction or lack of quality guidance. Hence, the author cannot be held liable for any liability, damages, reparation any monetary loss incurred directly or indirectly by the recipient reader.

The author owns all copyright to the document and information contained therein and is not held by the publisher or freelancer.

All trademarks and brands within this book are for clarifying purposes only and are owned by the owners themselves, not affiliated with this document.

Contents

Chapter 1

Introduction to tantric sex

"When you are in love, sex catapult from being casual to emotional; at this point, the sexual connection becomes a great tool for bonding."

The truth is that the body knows what it wants, and it is our duty to find out more about that for great satisfaction. Body urges, and desires are often a vast world to explore. As simple as it may seem, a good understanding of your body's sexual desires can drive the great passion that takes you to body and mind fulfillment. That is the focus of this book; to help you feel you. If you are looking in this direction, tantric sex may be best to achieve the desired result

Tantric sex is a sexual yoga that features the capturing and impacting properties of regular yoga exercise but in a sexual manner. With proper understanding, you can achieve a beautiful erotic moment that allows you to stay awake and feel the process of having sex with your significant other.

It is not always easy to find the right person who makes you feel greatly awake, but you learn to explore your body better when you meet the right person. I often believe a great relationship or love life is built essentially on this. If you take a moment to check our topic again, you will realize that this is never about casual sex. It is about driving the greatest passion in your body and eventually finding peace with the right person.

Believe me when I say this will not happen with every person you meet; however, a proper understanding of your body helps you know it is happening and when it is not. So let's take a walk far away from the casual sex that only drain you emotionally. In this book, we will learn about building a connection with your body and maximizing your emotions for sexual exploration without holding back.

This is all about you and me trying to find peace with our inner selves and understanding that our bodies love certain things better than others. If you want to know someone who makes you feel connected the most, then understanding what connection, sexual and emotional, means to your body is the first step. If you are ready to take this with me, I hope we enjoy this journey more than expected.

For a healthy relationship, tantric sex is everything and more. I understand other important aspects of things and other needs or lists to be checked. However, you cannot be in a relationship or proceed to check any list if you do not find a sincere connection within you and with the person. Yet, nothing connects two people romantically more than sex. So, instead of casual sex, I'll say go for a good one!

This is not a guide or manual on how to have tantric sex. It is a book aimed at connecting you with the greatest passion you carry and helping you find good orgasms and sexual satisfaction. The impact of this is enormous and cannot be sufficiently captured in words. You open a new world, see yourself better, and see your partner from the best perspective with a proper understanding.

So if you are planning on building a healthy relationship or love life with someone, or you are planning on understanding your sexual desires a little deeper, grab a seat and do not leave a page unread. By reading, you will understand that deriving the greatest sexual pleasure comes with added benefits that make life generally better.

This book is divided into carefully planned chapters to help you properly understand the concept. It starts by helping you understand the idea behind tantric sex. Following that, we will examine several benefits of tantric sex.

Chapter 3 of this book will help you develop connections using several body parts to create a rapport that eventually gets your body ready for more than casual sex. This is followed by chapter 4, where we talked about securities in both genders.

The book will progress with other chapters that help you through tantric sex. This includes creating a vivid understanding of types of penetration, orgasm, and the role of sexually-oriented body parts. And finally, we will examine a few sex positions to explore.

Chapter 2

The therapeutic nature of tantric sex

Tantra is not like the regular or casual sex that lets you reach orgasm and end. It goes deeper to inform your body new level of satisfaction, connection, and intimacy resulting in positive impacts like therapeutic benefits.

Yes, regular sex is beneficial to the body, but when you let your body feel every part of this amazing moment, you feel a new level of ecstasy rather than mere orgasm.

Tantric sex primarily urges individuals to zero in on mind-body associations. This can prompt satisfying sexual encounters and more extraordinary closeness. Its purpose is to circulate sexual energy throughout the body for healing, transformation, and inspiration.

Therapeutic benefits of tantric sex

- **Get healing from sexual trauma**

Healing from sexual trauma can be a little hard for victims. Situations like rape, sexual harassment, and sexual objectification deal with our self-esteem in a way that we do not expect. When someone is sexually traumatized, they may be unable to engage in sexual activities because it reminds them of bad memories. The negativity may surpass being remembered, and a person can get anxious or scared at the idea of having sex.

Tantric sex is one of the best ways to help someone through this situation. It helps eliminate shame and work by gradually turning the victim on and leading them t to believe their partners.

Tantric sex enables people to become more aware and in touch with their own bodies. One can incorporate one's body's desire during sex with a partner by understanding one's desire. This could lead to more intense orgasms and increased sexual contentment.

It also facilitates our awareness of this connectivity. We make the unconscious visible. Suppressed emotions and feelings are stored in the body. It's a big burden that affects how you connect with others daily. Tantric healing allows repressed emotions and sensations to be released. The body begins to unwind and feel secure. The door to experiencing connection, freedom, and joy is now open. This benefit of tantra is suitable for people dealing with emotional barriers to self-touch. To maximize the benefits, it is advisable to move at your own pace without blaming yourself.

Take time through the pleasure and internalize it; the more you do this, the more you are likely to heal. An ideal sex position for this is the snake trap pose. Since it allows for close rapport, the traumatized partner can get needed reaffirmation that tells them they are engaging in this lovely activity with the right person. It also feels them with so much care and orgasm and does not cause pain or discomfort. These are the right energies for someone trying to move on

The Snake trap Pose

Engage in a snake trap for more shallow and soft penetration, allowing you to feel the whole of your body in the process. The pose also enhances whispering or communication, emotional intimacy, eye contact, and body view

How to do: Follow the yab yum procedure with simple changes like legs intertwined to form a V shape. Enhance stability by placing your hand on the other person's ankle.

- **It eases stress and prevents anxiety**

We all deal with tense situations, and getting through life alone can affect our mental health; however, spending time with your loved ones will allow you to pass the time most effectively and blissfully. One of such way is through tantra.

Tantric sexual activity can ease your body, help you forget about your daily troubles and anxiety, and release various hormones beneficial to your general health.

Your body releases endorphins and oxytocin during sex, which produce sensations of relaxation and connection as this helps to prevent anxiety and despair.

It also increases dopamine, a neurotransmitter known as the "feel-good hormone" because it reinforces pleasurable experiences. One of the most effective tantric sex positions for this effect is the Lap Top pose

The Lap Top Pose

The lap top enhances eye contact and provides support with one of the partner's hands, making it great for a lovely experience. Another good side is that the penetration can be deeper, giving room for a wilder orgasm, and you can feel each other breath which complements eye contact and increases rapport.

How to do this

The penetrating partner will sit on a large chair with a pillow placed under their knees for elevation. Ensure that the chair is large and strong enough to carry two people. The receiving partner will then straddle the penetrating partner and maintain a lower stretch onto the penetrating partner. Once the penetration occurs, the receiving partner slowly moves her legs over the penetrating partner's shoulder and rests on the back of the chair.

For balance, the penetrating partner will need to support receiving partner with their hand. This ensures that the receiving partner can continuously rock the penetrating partner. The penetrating partner can enhance deeper thrust by slightly pulling her hip up and down.

- **Awakening your sexual energy to flow freely within your body**

When the sexual energy is high enough, your eyes may mist up or cry, but don't stop the motion or break the interaction by laughing or chatting about something else. Having blissful moments indicates you've awakened an enormous sexual force you've never felt before. At this point, you should not just stop; instead, try something easy and fun like the ship pose.

The Ship Pose

There is no better option for more fun when tired or a little lazy. Spending some time doing the ship pose instead of cuddling can also be more effective. Also, since this is all about building bonds and creating a better sexual life for you and your partner, enjoying this pose will be beneficial.

How to do this:

Let the penetrating partner lie on their back, and the receiving partner sit on them with their legs on the same side.

Both parties face the same direction as the receiving partner completely controls the penetration.

- **Long intercourse that enhances relaxation and helps heal depression**

Tantric sex is the same as a regular quickie. It is often a long hour of sex that allows you to gradually move from one position or stage to another, giving room for intense lovemaking and the formation of deeper connection.

While these are beneficial to both parties and your love life, tantra also increases the calmness and relaxation you feel. In this regard, you will be sexually satisfied without burning energy.

If you are dealing with depression or related mental health, this is a way to free the mind from all the worries and enjoy the moment with your spouse.

For this purpose, a combination of multiple sex positions is effective. You can try as many as possible but never forget to keep it within your partner's preferences. Here are a few options to explore.

1. The Rowing Boat Pose

The rowing boat pose is one sex position that establishes gradual trust between partners. It allows you to get into an exciting sex position and keep the fun and bonding intact.

How to do this:

The penetrating partner will lie on their back, and the receiving partner will gently sit on the penis, allowing penetration. Once penetration occurs, the man will sit up slowly and brings his knees and torso up. The receiving partner and the man will face each other; the receiving partner will then bend their knee up and wrap their legs around the man.

Both parties will slip their hands under each other's knee and hold firmly for balance.

2. The Eagle Pose

Everyone can enjoy the eagle pose as no flexibility is required. It is also an easy pose that does not make you uncomfortable yet remains impressive as required.

How to do this:

The position starts with the receiving partner lying on the bed with their knees slightly bent up. The penetrating partner then bends his knee at the edge of the bed facing the receiving partner. The man will grab the receiving partner's ankles and raise her legs for penetration.

3. The Star Pose

Like other tantric sex positions, the star pose is also good for bonding and pleasurable sex. it fills the moment with urges without rushing to orgasm.

How to do this:

The receiving partner will lie on their back, bending one leg up and laying the other flat on the surface. The penetrating partner then sits in between the receiving partner's leg and penetrates softly.

4. The Triumph Arch Pose

The triumph act pose is a complex yet enjoyable sex pose that allows the man to fondle the woman's breast and pave the way for greater orgasm for the woman. It is ideal for women who like their partners to play with their breasts for more fun. However, it is only recommended if you consider yourself more flexible.

How to do this:

The receiving partner will sit by kneeling down while the penetrating partner sits with his leg stretched between the receiving partner's thighs. The receiving partner will lean backward, lying on the penetrating partner's leg for deep penetration and thrusting. With this, the man can caress the receiving partner's breast and touch her softly to heighten orgasm.

Chapter 3

Important factors in a rapport

Building rapport with your partner is essential or tantric sex because both parties must be present in the moment. Hence, it is not a one-partner thing.

Yes, it is ok to find what works for you, but there is a need to touch and look at each other in ways that get you sensitive the most. This is what gets the body ready for the moment.

Understand that tantric sex is not about the sex itself; it creates a moment that you feel deeper in your body and aids your bonding. So the focus is not on how fast you get to it but on how effective the process is for you and your partner. For this purpose, a deep connection is required. However, you do not need to force a particular way on each other; just examine the options below and do what works best.

3.1   Eye contact

Eye gazing or maintaining eye contact is powerful that can heighten intimacy but can be a little overwhelming at the start. These simple activities communicate deeper with the other person and send some message into your sense. However, it can be impossible at the start but may get better with practice.

Erotic moments are often characterized by vulnerability, an aspect of our lives that cannot be eliminated but is hard to accept. When you are having sex with your partner, there is a chance that you do not want to maintain eye contact because you are concerned about looking vulnerable to them. So you may decide to look away.

However, when you can boldly look them right in the eyes, you develop a connection based on trust and confidence. You want to comfortably be with them without any fear. Your partner becomes one of the few people you subconsciously allow to see your vulnerabilities. The more your practice this, the better it becomes, and the more you enjoy sex and bond with your partner.

3.2   Breathing

As mentioned earlier, tantric exercise is sexual yoga; hence, certain tips for yoga exercise apply, and one of them is conscious breathing. During tantric sex, breathing allows you to stay present in the moment. You are lying down satisfying your partner's desire; you are interested in getting the right satisfaction and connection. Also, conscious breathing can enhance relaxation, which helps you enjoy the moment. It also improves energy flow allowing you to rhyme with your body's desire.

The most important impact of this is the ability to stay conscious and understand body exploration. Tantric sex practice focus on helping you build a strong connection with your partner, giving you the "no one touches me like him or her vibe." However, the only way to understand and appreciate this is by staying present in the moment. You discover more things about your body and sex, and your love life also gets better every day.

3.3   Communication

When you are with someone who sees your vulnerability but loves you the same, the feeling is good, and you just want to reciprocate it. While that may be in the moment, consistent practice will eventually help you develop permanent and sincere feelings toward each other.

Communication is everything in a relationship. It is also effective for tantric sex and can be done in several ways. By merely touching your partner, you may be sending a message to them. Yes, it all depends on how your touch them. Caressing your partner shows just how much you want to take time to know their body. Enough foreplay can do more exploration than just going to the act, and yes, words are effective too.

Believe me, when I say communicating during sex will improve your love life. During sex, there is a need to communicate with your partner. Telling them how much the moments and how much you love them. As you explore each other's bodies, it will serve a better purpose to let them know what you like the best and how you feel at the moment.

The power of words in this regard cannot be underestimated; it comes with the ability to improve your feelings in general.

If you explore tantric sex alone, you can communicate without saying a word; by acknowledging the moment, you are getting to know your body. With that, you can achieve a great orgasm without anyone.

3.4   Awareness (consciousness)

When it comes to tantra, awareness is everything. Staying conscious and enjoying the moment is the desired result. For this purpose, body and mind awareness is important to achieve the best result.

You learn a lot during tantric sex, so focus on your partner and pay quality attention to your body. As you progress from one point to another, caress each other or change position, and be in the moment so you get to feel every part of it.

One good way to achieve this is eye gazing. By looking at the next person, you are not only telling them that you trust them, but you are also paying attention to different changes, and your mind does not get to wander far away from the moment.

You can do this through kissing. Also, ensure that the body exploration is not done by one person, so switch roles from time to time and consciously learn about each other.

3.5   Relaxation

Tantric sex is not a race to an orgasm, so do not rush through this. Take time to stay calm and relaxed at the moment. Understand that this is not casual sex for mere sexual satisfaction. Here, you want to learn about your partner's sexual urges and your body's desires.

Taking it slow to ensure that you do not hurt each other is an impressive one to go about things. You need to feel connected physically and emotionally to your partner. You want to do this when you are relaxed and in a good mood.

Tantric sex will not lead to a fast orgasm, so you enjoy it better when you are more relaxed. The more you get passionate, the more time you want to explore each other's bodies.

Tantra also promotes calmness, so if you are anxious about having sex, it can help you take proper control of this. And with that, you become more confident about your sex life. This is a more effective way for women to control anxiety or shyness during sex. It can also be useful for men in the same way.

Relaxation also lets you pay attention to your sense organs. As you calmly explore each other sexually, you begin to understand what being with this person feels like. How kissing them tastes and how they moan during sex.

One good benefit is that this lets you know if you feel right by being with this person. In this regard, an effective love-building mechanism prevents you from staying with someone you are not comfortable with without knowing.

Here are two sex positions to enhance rapport

1. The Lustful Leg Pose

For the best tantric sex experience, a position that allows you to face your partner is ideal, hence, the lustful leg is one of the options to go for. Though it can be a little complex and should not practice unless you are ready to push off your limit a little, it is an exciting sex experience to enjoy with your partner.

How to do this:

The penetrating and receiving partners will face each other at approximately a shoulder-width apart. The receiving partner will then place one leg on the bed while the penetrating partner leans to bring his shoulder under the receiving partner's leg. The receiving partner can rest their leg on the shoulder for balance.

The receiving partner will lean back a little and wrap their arms around the penetrating partner's neck. The penetrating will slowly straighten up, holding the receiving partner's waist while penetrating them slowly.

2. Ascent to Desire pose

As its name implies, this position fills you with more passion for each other's bodies. You can feel every part of your partner, and they can feel you too. The main point here is that the connection is strongly maintained because you support each other. This can be a little tiring, but it is a lovely sexual experience that can be enjoyed.

How to do this:

This tantra pose begins with the penetrating partner standing on their feet with their hip-width apart and bends leg a little. They lift the receiving partner up, and the receiving partner will wrap their legs around the penetrating partner's waist. The receiving partner then puts their legs on the bed to provide support.

Chapter 4

Sexual insecurities

Sexual insecurity is not a gender-based idea because it affects anyone. However, feeling sexually insecure can affect a healthy relationship drastically. There is a need to feel like you compliment your partner equally, and when it comes to sex, you just do not want the idea of not being enough.

So even when your spouse is not complaining, there is a chance that you are feeling insecure. This is particularly true for women who have to deal with gaining experience and participating actively in sex to enhance satisfaction.

For men, sexual insecurity can be real and can eventually affect sexual performance. Our society puts more heavyweight on men that feeling sexually insecure is often a problem more men deals with. However, taking control and not appearing weak forces them to hide this so well as they battle with it alone.

-       **For men**

Men are often interested in getting their partners to the climax of orgasm. It is an act that is considered masculine but can be harmful when one dwells too much on it. Often insecurities are hidden under the façade of caring for your partner, but in the real sense, it points to fragility and the requirement for help.

Though sexual insecurities appear in everyone, masculinity is more connected to sexual capabilities. The inability to meet this requirement can heighten insecurity in men. Men are more concerned about their sexual performances than women. Our current society demoralizes men who cannot sexually satisfy their partners.

Sexual insecurities may lead to anxiety and several other mental health conditions putting men in an awkward condition where it becomes hard to see for help. They may be insecure about their penis size, general performance, or ability to please their spouse.

No one wants to feel this way, so you should not be dealing with this alone. Start by understanding that you've done nothing wrong to deserve this. The ability to overcome this problem does rely on your hand alone. A lot must be put in place, so you should never take the blame or suffer in silence.

Though sexual insecurities may appear in men at different ages, these disorders are typical, and natural components of the aging process do not exonerate men from the stigma.

4.1   Impotence or Erectile Dysfunction (ED)

Erectile dysfunction or impotence occurs when a man cannot get an erection or keep one long enough to achieve sexual satisfaction. This affects both parties since the inability of a man to keep or get an erection means low sexual performance.

Statistically, above 30million men globally deal with impotence. Almost all male adults experience ED once in a while; however, some deal with it more often. Thankfully, this situation can improve with time and the right help.

Causes of Erectile Dysfunction

Several things can lead to erectile dysfunction in men from medical factors to psychological factors. This problem often occurs in older men, but this is not an affirmation that younger men are not dealing with the problem. However, an older man has a higher tendency to develop ED since age can affect how easily a man gets aroused.

When you are unable to get an erection, there is a chance that you are experiencing improper or blocked blood flow. This happens when blood flow is disturbed from passing through the blood vessels to the penis.

On the other hand, the inability to keep an erection implies that the penis is erected but is unable to keep an erection for as long as desired. This implies the presence of a faulty vein causing the draining of blood from the penis.

Other causes of impotence include hormonal imbalance, high consumption of drugs, and other medicines recommended for other illnesses.

Aside from this, impotence is caused by psychological problems. This is the most prevalent cause of this problem in younger men. When men deal with sexual insecurities, health issues like erectile dysfunction can be one way this insecurity affects them and eventually result in anxiety.

Similarly, impotence is linked to the lack of communication on sexual needs and satisfaction. This may eventually heighten the insecurities. This is where tantric sex can be a lot helpful. By putting your mind at ease, you get to stimulate a great desire within, and there is a strong drive capable of getting you into the mood. Since the gentle process, you can trigger different body parts in harmony. Gradual response to your body needs and the consciousness practice you will engage in during tantric sex will set your body in motion. You may be surprised as to how better you perform sexually.

4.2   Premature Ejaculations

Premature ejaculation is another symptom of sexual insecurity in men. It happens when a man experiences orgasm before intercourse or a few minutes after you start. It should be noted that ejaculation during sex is a normal thing; however, this must be followed by an erection that allows you to continue the sex and get satisfaction. So it is only an issue when you ejaculate and lose erection.

Premature ejaculation can be caused by several things, and lack of sexual chemistry between partners is one major cause. If you are experiencing this, exploit tantric sex to overcome it.

Tantric sex captures the power of will and the ability to control one's body. Hence, you can communicate better with your body and partner by engaging in it. This is not a miracle expected to be effective the first time. Still, consistent practicing can be very helpful to get your body in the mood and retain an erection even after ejaculating.

For women

Sexual insecurity in women is almost similar to that of men. It also prevents you from sexually satisfying your partner. Women also feel the panic of not being sexually enough or capable. The idea of your partner tagging you as 'bad in bed' can be more heartbreaking than you imagine.

However, unlike men who actually have to deal with premature ejaculation or impotence, women deal with sexual insecurities resulting in the ability to last long during sex or reach orgasm easily and not being able to pick your body up again. This can also affect your relationship, and in most cases, developing genuine affection toward your partner can be an effective way of dealing with this problem

Tantra will be helpful in this regard because it focuses on building your emotion and passion. Body exploration allows you to discover new things about yourself. This may include learning about your G-spots and things that turn on. It also helps develop the right passion that lets you stay in the moment, want more of the erotic moment, and eventually derive satisfaction that feels so unique that you want to do it again.

Also, shyness or inability to be bold about your sexual needs can cause sexual insecurity in women. Where this is the case, tantric sex is an effective tool to use. By engaging in communication and eye gazing, you can overcome the fear of being vulnerable, opening the door to a better sexual exploration.

4.3   Signs of sexual insecurities in women

- Inability to feel your G-spot
- Lack of confidence to inform your partner of your sexual needs.
- Getting satisfied or reaching orgasm faster than you want

Chapter 5

Getting ready (for a tantric experience in bed)

As noted earlier, tantra is an exercise of the mind as much as the body; getting your mind prepared is as vital as getting physically prepared. Therefore, clear your mind of all fear, doubts, and overconfidence. Don't be too eager, but prepare a union of your mind, soul, and spirit. Make sure everything around you is quiet and calm, and no troubling thoughts are running through you at the moment. A few minutes of meditation can help get your mind in the right state of readiness.

At this stage, it is good to focus on your breathing. Start by taking a few deep breaths and connecting with what's going on in your mind, whether stress or eagerness to do what you are about to do.

Stretch for a while. Clear your mind of running thoughts as you stretch each arm and leg. Even people who have a lot of things to unpack from their minds will feel lighter as they follow this process.

Tantra is a holistic practice, which means that you must also prepare your surrounding space before beginning. Your environment reasonably affects your state of mind and your capacity to relax and enjoy the ride ahead of you. It is the pathway to getting there and more important than having a good time with sex or Orgasm.

To make your environment conducive to tantric sex, make sure the following conditions are put in place:

•   Make sure the temperature in your space is at a suitable level. If it's freezing outside, turn on the heat an hour before your practice to ensure that your room is comfortable and heated before you begin. During the summer, turn on the air conditioner, but keep the temperature at or above 70 degrees so that the space is cool but not frigid.

•   Using candles or colored light bulbs, you can create a calming atmosphere. Light from candles will provide a romantic touch to the room, while soft red lighting will add a passionate touch to the room.

•   Fill the room with the aroma of your choosing. Lighting a fragrant candle, diffusing essential oil, burning incense sticks, or hanging flowers can add to the ambiance. Choose a scent that makes you feel sexy but isn't overwhelming.

•   Make your room more welcoming. You can also lay out a satin throw blanket and a couple of soft cushions on the floor to achieve this.

The overall goal is to create a sensual or romantic atmosphere by all peaceful means possible. Another point that helps a lot here is playing some music that you can dance to, either by yourself or with a partner; by following all the steps highlighted, you would have set everything needed in motion.

Soft penetration

Many think that having a strong penis and thrusting hard is important for the real action during sex, but with tantric sex, it is possible to think it the other way round. In fact, "size doesn't matter," and "even a small figurine can play a big show." Ordinarily, It may seems like the truth is that you need a hard penis to get into the tight and firmly closed female sexual organ is. Still, the truth is that "soft penetration," when done correctly, can be more intense for both of you.

It makes no difference how large or little your organ is; this method, which originates in tantric teachings, is acceptable for everyone, including "small figurines." The vast majority of men believe that only a hard thrust can satisfy their partner's needs. Ladies, on the other hand, mostly love it calmer.

It is not a common woman's dream to have sex with a man, as she may see in a sex or porn film scenario. Those are usually scripted, with the first sexual contact between the main characters usually comprised of the following: blouse ripping, pinning the woman against the wall, intense kissing of her cheeks and jaw... all in 5 seconds. Afterward, she is flung to the ground or thrown over the table. As a high point, he makes a couple of fast thrusts on her, and they both happily roll from side to side.

Despite the satisfaction, this might give the watcher, in reality, she is unable even to get wet, let alone achieve the game's climax in such a short period. If you have seen this in the movie, you need to get rid of that mentality to have a softcore tantra experience.

The method of soft penetration can also treat many types of sexual problems. For men, it can be problems with getting an erection or having an early ejaculation. For women, this method can help them become more aware of the sensitivity of their genitals.

"Soft penetration" is all about how to put the penis in the vagina without it getting an erection. Yes, we can hear your screams. It's not going to happen! Everyone has never heard of it! But many couples (maybe even threesomes) decided to work on their relationships and try new tantric techniques.

They heard about it and tried it. You can get a very good soft penetration by following these steps one by one:

Giving due regard to Romance

Prepare for a romantic evening, morning, or lunchtime, depending on your preferences. Turn off your phones, dim the lights, light candles, fill your bath with warm water, turn on soothing, romantic music (make sure it doesn't stop in the middle of the "process"), and prepare delicious food and drinks (alcohol is not suggested), and so on. This implies that you must set aside a few hours of your time. The absolute bare minimum is two hours. It is also important that the room is not too cold. Keep the temperature minimally warm.

Undressing

Prepare yourself and your partner by taking off your clothes. Take the shirt, bra, panties, and trousers as gently as possible. Be gentle and do not rush the process, by the way. Undressing does not have to be done strictly; it can be done in a brief striptease.

Get to stroking

Be mindful of this stage; it should not be thoughtless or sensual stroking but rather relaxing and loosening touches that help you relax and unwind. It's critical to have warm hands when working. If they are cold, it is sufficient to massage each other's hands together for a short period.

Note that It is not recommended to use massage oils since the touches are too intense and result in excessive erotic hype. And that is not your intention. You'll get to the most crucial part: DO NOT GET YOUR HANDS ON THE MOST SENSITIVE AREAS.

The most sensitive part of the body does not always mean the penis, nipples, or clitoris. Some persons have sensitive earlobes, buttocks, and scruffs as sensitive as more normal regions. Shortly put, erogenous zones are off-limits during this stage.

Other regions should be stroked as gently as possible for at least 30 minutes. Neither 10 nor 15, but at the very least 30. Transform your thinking into the mindset of "I'm doing this for myself, not because of any particular "style of operation."

It should be a time filled with affection, when you may take a break and allow yourself the luxury of experiencing the experience of "now and here." It's best not to say anything and instead direct your partner's attention away from the extreme enthusiasm or excessive eagerness.

Hard penetration

Finally, there is the actual penetration. If stroking induces an erection in a man's penis, the stroking should be stopped until the erection is gone. Replace that with some pleasant and tender common memories.

Take four deep breaths in and four deep breaths out, eat something delicious, and so on. When everything has returned to normal, begin with so-called spooning, the cuddling of two spoons. The male lies behind the woman, and both lie on their sides. Then he takes a soft penis in his hand and softly presses its end into the vagina as deeply as possible. To provide her partner access to her vagina, the woman opens her legs apart a little (ben done leg or places a pillow between her knees).

Both settle down in the spooning position with care, focusing on the penis remaining in the vagina. The fact you have to do nothing but breathe and waiting can be a little overwhelming; however, do not forget that you are doing this for yourself. The more time you have, the better.

The man can try to insert his penis farther into the vagina while they are waiting – slowly, with his hand. The majority of the time, it's difficult to wait for even a second longer so that you may get started! And so, what exactly are you waiting for. You are waiting to achieve a complete erection of the penis!

The majority of the time, it's difficult to wait for even a second longer so that you may get started! However, do not attempt to roleplay the Duracell rabbit or a dog encountering a bitch in heat too quickly. Instead, take pleasure in every second of it, feel every centimeter of the insertion; after all, he has earned it!

Usually, a woman is so excited before she even feels the initial movement that she cannot tell when an orgasm has occurred. There is no limit to time at this stage, and it is not required to last 45 minutes or 30 minutes. Follow the instructions, complete all of the activities, and you'll be good.

Once you are good with the mood and you've enjoyed caressing each other's body, give your partner their first orgasm with a landslide pose that features gentle yet deep thrusting sex to keep the mood alive. Ensure they are fully in the mood to prevent them from getting tired. This is not to end the moment; hence it must be introduced when you feel your partner is fully awake and ready.

- **The Landslide Pose**

The landslide pose is another great tantric sex position to try out as you explore your partner's body for emotional and sexual satisfaction. Consider that little flexibility is required for this pose and should only be tried if you love to enjoy new sex positions that are not similar to yab yum or missionary.

How to do this:

The receiving partner will lie on their stomach for the landslide position, placing their legs straight and slightly apart behind them. The penetrating partner will then sit behind the receiving partner placing his leg in his front and leaning back a little or at 45 degrees. The penetrating partner will support himself with his hand as he penetrates the receiving partner. There is enough room for a deeper thrust, and the receiving partner can close their legs tightly for fit penetration.

Chapter 6

Orgasm - Introduction and Explanation

When you reach the pinnacle of sexual arousal, you will experience an orgasm. It's usually a really pleasant sensation. To experience an orgasm — also known as a cum or climax — you must first experience sexual tension increasing until it reaches a peak, which releases pressure in your body and genitals.

The way our body reacts to Orgasm differs from person to person, but there are common physical markers of Orgasm that you should look out for. Your genitals and other parts of your body will experience an extremely powerful and wonderful sensation, which will last for several hours. Every 5-8 seconds, the muscles in your vagina or penis and your anus contract (squeeze) roughly once per second. Your heartbeat and breathing rate both increase as well.

During an orgasm, the penis normally squirts a small amount of semen (cum) into the cervix, referred to as ejaculation (or ejaculation). It is possible to Orgasm without ejaculating, and it is also possible to ejaculate without having an orgasm, but they are more likely to occur together.

Before and during an orgasm, it is usual for your vagina to become extremely moist. It's also possible for fluid to squirt or drip out of your vulva before or during an orgasm (this is sometimes called female ejaculation or squirting). This isn't a puddle of pee. In general, people ejaculate more from their vulva than from their penis. Note also that ejaculation from either site is completely natural and completely normal.

It's important to look into the idea of Orgasm in tantric sex, especially when a delayed Orgasm can be mistaken for a tantric Orgasm, which isn't always the case. However, it is an important part.

When you have sex, you can keep Orgasm from coming by sending sexual energy through your body instead of letting it out at the height of the encounter. When it comes to having more power and stamina, many tantric couples will say that keeping this energy around is a good thing, and many will say it feels great.

The main goal of tantric sex is not to get orgasms. Instead, the goal is to pay attention to every sensation felt during the contact, both when giving and receiving.

The more you pay attention and immerse yourself in the experience, the more energy and connection you will have with your partner.

The gift of good health can be given to your partner during sex. They say it's important to get the most out of your sexual energy to stay healthy and happy, but not everyone agrees with this.

Sexual activity has been shown to help people deal with stress and raise serotonin levels. Nothing could be more profound or relaxing than this level of care.

Some tantric lovers have shown that they can stay in semi-orgasmic ecstasy for a long time. However, they can stay in this state of mind for several minutes or even hours. Tantric enthusiasts who know how to climax can do this for a long time. Once you learn how to have a long orgasm, you'll be able to have a lot of orgasms with your husband or wife.

a.   Orgasm is spiritual

During an orgasm, the knowledge of one's own identity or ego is completely lost. Therefore you can connect with your eternal nature. To achieve higher levels of consciousness, sex and Orgasm have traditionally been employed as instruments in spiritual practice. Orgasm is, in reality, one of the practices that can be used to achieve enlightenment, according to certain sources. Tantra is the most well-known example of sexual practice employed as a doorway to enlightenment. It is also the most widely practiced.

"Human life on Earth is a by-product of orgasm." even though it appears too good to be true, this idea holds up well. "Human lid conception are index

b.   Men and women are not the same

Generally, the differences between male and female orgasms include that the climax in the female response can be held back for quite longer than the male response. By this, we mean it might take more time for females to Orgasm than males, and the release of semen usually accompanies the male response; momentary muscular contractions accompany both male and female orgasms, but the female response's effects are typically more prolonged.

Also, because male reactions are typically obvious more quickly than female responses, the male likely reaches orgasms more consistently during intercourse than the female; on the other hand, following Orgasm, the female is more likely to remain sexually excited for a longer period. She may experience numerous successive orgasms, whereas the male is more likely to experience a second orgasm only after some time has passed since the first.

c.   Breasts and the vagina's role in orgasms

The role of the breast (The nipple) and vagina in women's Orgasm can never be overemphasized.

Nipples are delightful little breast berries available in various sizes, shapes, and colors. When used properly, they can induce a stirring orgasmic response. However, although the nipple orgasm is a rare species in the orgasm lexicon, it does exist.

What distinguishes the nipple orgasm from other forms of genital stimulation is that it does not require any other genital stimulation to reach a climax. To induce breast orgasm, it is necessary to gently stimulate the breast area by rubbing and caressing it in a circular motion.

Make sure you don't touch the nipple until it has grown pointy and difficult to manipulate. After that, suck and softly pinch with a feather-like touch to finish the process. Don't forget that the trick is to take it slow and appreciate the pleasure as it comes, rather than expecting the Orgasm to be a means to another purpose.

As for the vagina, it is called Yoni, which means "sacred space" in Sanskrit. In tantric philosophy, the vagina is treated with the utmost love and respect, so yoni massage is a way to show the vagina owner how much you love and respect them.

The psychological and spiritual cervix is at the heart of the vaginal Orgasm. It's a full-blown, no-holds-barred orgasm. The energy of orgasm moves through the center of your spine to your heart. It feels more like a deep bass drum than sex.

Take a deep breath and put your body in a relaxed, comfortable place. Make a whispering sound by constricting the back of your throat, then inhale again and let that sound out again. Take deep, slow, audible breaths all the time.

This helps you spread the orgasmic energy all over your body. People who have this type of Orgasm do not want the energy just in their clitoris. They want it all over their bodies as well. People who breathe deeply can help move that energy from the vagina to all parts of their bodies.

d.   Orgasm in women

Women can experience Orgasm in a variety of ways, one of which is briefly described in the four steps below:

1. A feeling of anticipation:

In this state of desire or arousal, the woman initiates or agrees to sexual activity. As the sexual encounter progresses, she notices that she concentrates primarily on the sexual stimuli. Blood begins to engorge the clitoris, vagina, and nipples, resulting in a full-body sexual blush over the entire body. The rate of her heartbeat and blood pressure rises. These processes are aided by the hormone testosterone and neurotransmitters such as dopamine and serotonin.

2. A plateau stage:

The rate of her heartbeat, blood pressure, and respiration are all increasing. This is a precursor to Orgasm; sexual tension increases in the body. According to researchers, due to this engorgement with blood, the outer one-third of the vagina becomes known as the "orgasmic platform, " The intense concentration on sexual impulses drowns out all other sensations.

3. Orgasm:

The uterus, vagina, and pelvic floor muscles go through cyclic contractions simultaneously. It is possible that muscles throughout the body contract due to the release of sexual tension induced by lovemaking or self-stimulation. A sensation of warmth that begins from the pelvis and travels across the entire body is commonplace.

In the final stage, her body relaxes as blood begins to flow away from the engorged genital organs. Blood pressure, heart rate, and breathing all return to normal after a brief period of fluctuation. This marks the end of Orgasm in women.

e.   Ejaculation is not an Orgasm for men

While Orgasm and ejaculation are frequently experienced simultaneously, they are two distinct events that must not necessarily occur simultaneously to be considered simultaneous.

Ejaculation is used to describe how the penis squirts a little amount of semen (cum) into the cervix during an orgasm. Ejaculating can occur independently of having an orgasm and vice versa; nevertheless, the two events are more likely to occur simultaneously.

A man can easily release sperm under different circumstances. This might even occur without sexual arousals, such as a wet dream.

f.   Orgasm in Men

When men are aware of their sexuality, they're more likely to have multiple orgasms voluntarily. This means that you need to know how sexuality works inside your body.

Tantric techniques will help you have a lot of mind-blowing orgasms. They are called multiple body orgasms, and they will help you have a lot of orgasms without ejaculating.

Orgasms get better and better when you control your urge to ejaculate, making you will move toward a higher, more powerful one. The time you have set aside for this most pleasurable and enlightening experience with your partner is always worth it.

It's a good idea only to ejaculate after you are sure your partner is completely satisfied. Keep calm: she will give you clear signs when she is ready. If you have this kind of tantric Orgasm, I call it the Tantric Big O. It will be your best orgasmic experience, and your ejaculation will be stronger and longer.

Conscious lovemaking makes you more physically, emotionally, and spiritually loved, connected, and intimate with your partner. Your experience will be so powerful and intense that it will make you smile for days. An ejaculation that happens just because your body wants to release some sexual tension isn't as good as this.

To get this power of choice over ejaculation, you need to have a clear, strong goal and a real desire to practice; practice is very important. No matter how good you are at any sport, you get poor at it if you don't practice. Understanding how to do something and doing it repeatedly is what it takes to become a master at it.

So, it is recommended that you stick to the tantric positions recommended in more detail. Read over, practice, and practice over again. It is an art and not just meant to be learned; it is meant to be mastered through practice.

Chapter 7

Key sexual factors for the tantric Orgasm

### a.	Testicles

The position of the testicles in tantric Orgasm is very eminent, and this is evident in two practices we shall consider below. The first is testicular breathing, while the other is lingam massage.

Testicular breathing

It is time for you to picture your balls getting bigger when you inhale next! Imagine that they are filled with the rejuvenating energy of fresh air. As you exhale, imagine all the anger and frustration you have stored in your nuts leaving, and contract your testicles as you imagine the carbon dioxide leaving your body so that your testicles are squeezed. This is the idea of testicle breathing.

When you breathe through your testicles, you encourage a flow of "energy" through your body by contracting your muscles. This is a practice that comes from ancient knowledge about yoga.

Inhaling and exhaling through your nose and mouth, known as diaphragmatic breathing exercises, can help you feel less anxious by lowering blood pressure and heart rate; as those exercises do, testicle breathing offers similar benefits.

In addition, testicular breathing is also acclaimed to help with conditions like erectile dysfunction and premature ejaculation. Because you can't breathe through your balls, testicular breathing is more like doing Kegels while taking deep breaths. As you inhale, you pull your testicles up and inward, and as you exhale, you let them go down, all while picturing energy flow from your testes to your brain.

"Breathing" through your balls might seem a little far-fetched, but there may be some evidence that testicular breathing can be good for you, at least in the same way that meditative breathing can be good. People who are stressed out might be able to calm down for a moment by deep breathing. Testicular breathing could also be good because it makes you move your balls. In the same way, if you try to squeeze your balls, you're doing Kegels, which can strengthen your pelvic muscles and help your bladder, bowel, and sexual health. Besides, they're almost the same things to do, except that you are also thinking about your nuts with only one of them.

Lingam massage

As regards lingam massage, it is a type of tantric massage in which the penis is massaged. The goal of lingam massage isn't just to have sex. Instead, the goal is to have a meditative sexual and spiritual experience.

Tantric massage has been used for a long time to help people become more aware of their sexual and spiritual selves. Tantric massage therapy is about learning how to build up sexual energy to feel pure pleasure.

It comes from the Sanskrit word for "penis." It is a tantric practice where you massage your penis and the areas around your penis. At the same time, the penis and testicles are massaged, as are the anus and scrotum and the prostate. The goal of a lingam massage isn't just to get you to have sex. The goal is to have full-body sexual and spiritual pleasure.

The two ways to get a lingam massage are tantric masturbation and tantric massage with a partner. The person who has the penis can do it independently or with a partner. It can be done on its own or as a kind of "prelude" to having sex. For people who want to use this sacred practice for masturbation and energy development, follow the same steps below on yourself.

Relax the penis owner:

The first way is fragmented urination, which entails urinating in brief bursts with pauses. The delay must be long enough to stop the pee flow at each specific pause. While continuing your sexual acts, your whole body will be tingling, especially your spine. Strong energies will flow through it and give you a sense of thrill. These thrills are nothing more than the energy transmuted by the urinary sphincters.

It is recommended that you visualize this energy (these "thrills") and direct it up the spine to the center of your forehead.

You should adopt sexual positions that take pressure off your bladder to reduce the chances of urinating altogether during your tantric session. It is also recommended to reduce your weight if you are overweight and limit your sugar, caffeine, and alcohol intake. This is because they can easily irritate your bladder. Furthermore, several sex positions will be discussed in the coming chapter.

These simple lifestyle adjustments mentioned above and frequent pelvic floor muscle exercises can also lessen or eliminate the urge to pee during sex as a long-term measure.

c.   Special breathing

Breathing is an important part of your Orgasm, even though it doesn't seem very sexy. It's the key to orgasmic pleasure and consciousness for women and lasting longer for men. The sexual benefits of learning new, simple ways to breathe are huge, and they come right from your own body. It aids relaxation by breathing deeply into your belly and helps you focus on pleasure while increasing blood flow. It could be rightly said that Oxygen is what makes the "O" in Orgasm happen.

meditative breathing can be good. People who are stressed out might be able to calm down for a moment by deep breathing. Testicular breathing could also be good because it makes you move your balls. In the same way, if you try to squeeze your balls, you're doing Kegels, which can strengthen your pelvic muscles and help your bladder, bowel, and sexual health. Besides, they're almost the same things to do, except that you are also thinking about your nuts with only one of them.

Lingam massage

As regards lingam massage, it is a type of tantric massage in which the penis is massaged. The goal of lingam massage isn't just to have sex. Instead, the goal is to have a meditative sexual and spiritual experience.

Tantric massage has been used for a long time to help people become more aware of their sexual and spiritual selves. Tantric massage therapy is about learning how to build up sexual energy to feel pure pleasure.

It comes from the Sanskrit word for "penis." It is a tantric practice where you massage your penis and the areas around your penis. At the same time, the penis and testicles are massaged, as are the anus and scrotum and the prostate. The goal of a lingam massage isn't just to get you to have sex. The goal is to have full-body sexual and spiritual pleasure.

The two ways to get a lingam massage are tantric masturbation and tantric massage with a partner. The person who has the penis can do it independently or with a partner. It can be done on its own or as a kind of "prelude" to having sex. For people who want to use this sacred practice for masturbation and energy development, follow the same steps below on yourself.

Relax the penis owner:

Lean your penis partner back in a comfortable position. A pillow for their head or hip. Their legs should be wide apart with knees bent to allow simple access to their genitalia. Solicit deep breaths. This will help you relax more.

Breathe

In tantra, the focus is on the breath. Remember to use the Bliss Breath when giving your spouse a lingam massage: receive their arousal and pleasure energy on the inhale and send them loving energy on the exhale. This unique breathing has three advantages:

1.   You'll sense more worship, meditation, and mindfulness.

2.   It will help you comprehend your partner's feelings.

3.   It will increase your sexual intuition—you will know what your spouse desires without them asking.

Remind the penis owner to inhale deeply

Before you begin the lingam massage, take a Bliss Breath together. Taking a few deep breaths together will relax you and align your biorhythms. As you massage them, urge them to breathe deeply, relax, and enjoy the nice feelings.

Massage and lubricate the penis

You can also use your favorite massage oil. Before the good stuff, slide your hands up and down the thighs. This will also relax your partner. Let them know what you enjoy about what you see and feel.

Then comes the testicles, and massage them slowly. You can gently press or pull the testicles with your fingernails. You can also cup and caress them.

Touch the back of thighs, inner part of thighs, and perineum (the area between the testicles and anus). These areas should be thoroughly massaged. Note that People's preferences for touch vary widely here. Some have low sensitivity, while others are more sensitive or ticklish. It is fine to ask your spouse how they want their testicles touched before or during the touch.

Rub the shaft

After teasing the penis's surrounding parts, go on to the penis's shaft. The key is variety; gradually soften your hold. Alternatively, straight up and down strokes with twisting motions while changing from one to two hands. When using only one hand, switch in-between the right and left hands, don't just use and overstress a single hand.

Try to alternate pressure, speed, rhythm, and techniques in simpler terms. Alternate the shaft strokes from the root to the head. Once at the head, you can either continue straight up and down or twist from the base of the shaft to just below the penis. Also, make sure you start slowly, then quickly, then slowly again.

Avoid climaxing

Your partner may be excited and want to come now. You can tell whether they're about to Orgasm by their breathing, body movement, and moaning. Either stop doing what you're doing or slow down and remind them to breathe and ride the wave of orgasmic feelings. The penis may become semi-hard; just relax; that's part of the plan.

Stimulate the Sacred Spot externally

The prostate is between the bladder and the penis, a walnut-sized gland. It is delightful when properly aroused. Injecting your fingers or a prostate massage sex toy into the anus opens the prostate (through massaging the outside without penetration).

Start externally if your partner isn't used to it. Look for a pea-sized indentation between the testicles and the anus to discover the sacred spot. Gently inward Slow down and let your companion guide you under pressure.

Use a circular massaging motion. Push in with your fingers or knuckles, then back off and push in again. If your companion has a lot of hair, use additional oil to get to the region. Or better yet, shave them for easier access.

Sacred Spot Internal Stimulation

Ask your penis partner if they'd like to add an inside massage to the prostate massage. If they're game, massage their anus with massage oil. Begin by gently massaging the exterior of the anus with your fingers. Do not proceed with an unauthorized insertion of a finger. Ask if they want more.

If your partner is ready, lubricate their anus and your fingers. Make sure your nails are smooth. Begin by inserting only one fingertip at a time. Wiggle it to relax your lover. The prostate is 2 to 3 inches within the anus, closer to the front wall of the rectum so that you can put your finger(s) deeper.

Once there, softly move your finger side to side, up and down, or "milk" it with a come hither motion (s).

Because prostate massage with your fingers can be tough at times, many sex toy businesses now sell prostate massagers that you can use when you're ready to step it up.

End massage

You can end the massage with an ejaculation orgasm or proceed to soft intercourse. For semen retention, have your spouse hold all their juices as they learn to convert genital orgasms into full-body energy orgasms.

b.   Urine

Men and people with penises have an inbuilt system that prevents urinating when they are sexually stimulated; unfortunately, it is not the same with women. This implies that women may feel increased urinal urgency during tantric sex

The urge to pee during sexual arousal is more common than you believe. You should know that it is very normal to feel the urge to pee during a sexual act. And an estimated 60% of females experience the urge to pee during intercourse.

When it comes to female Orgasm, sometimes referred to as squirting Orgasm, the role of urine is more crucial. Squirting refers to the expulsion of fluid from the vagina during orgasms. Urine is ejected from the bladder quickly during this type of Orgasm. Orgasm squirting may not be common among folks who possess vaginal organs.

If, on the other hand, you wish to control urine while having tantric sex, there are a couple of ways to control peeing and make it blend with your sexual energy.

The first way is fragmented urination, which entails urinating in brief bursts with pauses. The delay must be long enough to stop the pee flow at each specific pause. While continuing your sexual acts, your whole body will be tingling, especially your spine. Strong energies will flow through it and give you a sense of thrill. These thrills are nothing more than the energy transmuted by the urinary sphincters.

It is recommended that you visualize this energy (these "thrills") and direct it up the spine to the center of your forehead.

You should adopt sexual positions that take pressure off your bladder to reduce the chances of urinating altogether during your tantric session. It is also recommended to reduce your weight if you are overweight and limit your sugar, caffeine, and alcohol intake. This is because they can easily irritate your bladder. Furthermore, several sex positions will be discussed in the coming chapter.

These simple lifestyle adjustments mentioned above and frequent pelvic floor muscle exercises can also lessen or eliminate the urge to pee during sex as a long-term measure.

c.   Special breathing

Breathing is an important part of your Orgasm, even though it doesn't seem very sexy. It's the key to orgasmic pleasure and consciousness for women and lasting longer for men. The sexual benefits of learning new, simple ways to breathe are huge, and they come right from your own body. It aids relaxation by breathing deeply into your belly and helps you focus on pleasure while increasing blood flow. It could be rightly said that Oxygen is what makes the "O" in Orgasm happen.

You need to be tense to have an orgasm, but you can feel a whole new thing when you relax these muscles. You might have felt sinus pressure, ringing in your ears, or just general pressure in your head after having sex. People have this happen when they hold their breath and tighten their muscles to Orgasm.

Breathing techniques can help you focus your mind and improve your blood flow, and they can also help you get into the "zone" of body/mind unity faster. These breathing techniques are simple but very effective. Check the following process on how to achieve Orgasm through breathing:

Step 1

Prepare by finding a comfortable seat and sitting up straight. Take regular deep breaths in and out to keep yourself calm and collected. Then purse your lips together as if you were sipping through a straw with your next inhalation. You may also adjust the airflow as it enters your vicinity.

Step 2

Take slow, deep breaths in, and contract your PC muscles at the bottom of your lungs as if you were blocking a pee stream. Please never give in to the temptation to clench your glutes all along.

Step 3

As you continue to inhale breath, imagine that you are zipping up your muscles around the energy rising from your spine, keeping them engaged as you go; after this, pull in the muscles of your lower abdominals while keeping your belly button sucked in.

Step 4

Draw your shoulders back and make sure your collarbones spread as you do so.

Step 5

Tuck your chin in and stretch the back of your neck while looking down gently at your feet. Once you have taken in enough air, seal your lips together and hold your breath while engaging all of the muscles along your spine.

To release, slightly open your mouth and visualize energy streaming from the crown of your head, down the front of your body, now softening each muscle group as it makes its way down.

Step 6

Relax your neck and shoulders muscles and allow your stomach to protrude. Also, take some time to relax your lower abdominal muscles.

Finally, let go of the PC muscles totally and allow yourself to relax. Note also that breath-work is a wonderful addition to any tantric practice since it can assist in strengthening the muscles on the pelvic floor, awaken stagnant energy in the body, and facilitate the transition into a meditative state. As a method of feeling centered, strong, and confident in my sexual energy in the mornings, I try to do this every morning. When I need to release my pelvic floor muscles, such as when I'm on my period or having pelvic pain, I do not perform this pose.

Another entirely different style is a woman straddling her man face to face with her heart, sacrum, and pelvis all touching. This is a cool way to show how powerful and connected we can be when doing orgasmic breath-work with a partner.

This is a good place to do the breathing exercises above. In this position, you are focused on your breathing, the skin of your partner, all of your senses, and most of all, being present with the love you feel for yourself, allowing this love to spread to your partner.

Immediately you and your partner sync in the same rhythm, and you can separate from this position. You can still touch each other, but give your Yoni and his penis with enough distance. Breathe, look at your partner with a beautiful gaze, and feel the energy from you and your partner simultaneously since the connection. Sense the breath. Arousal can flow where it needs to, and you can let it.

One of the best things about this experience is that it gives both partners a chance to be very present and watch the flow of the other person's Orgasm. It is a guide to how we like to masturbate, but it also gives us a different kind of intimate feeling than what we usually do.

d.   Nipples

One fascinating fact about nipples is that they are packed with nerve endings that make them ideal for pleasure. There are two ways to have a nipple orgasm: You can touch yourself or have it during tantric sex with a partner. Given that nipples are wired to the same part of the brain that receives information from the clitoris and vagina, it's no surprise that nipple orgasms are real.

When nipples are stimulated, one is overwhelmed by a feeling one happiness, furiousness, or even horny. The hypothalamus, which controls the brain chemicals that make us happy, is one of the structures in the brain that controls this stimulation. Activating the nipples makes the hypothalamus release oxytocin. This powerful neurohormone can boost feelings of bonding and make orgasms more pleasurable. To get a nipple orgasm during tantric sex, the following simplified steps may be explored:

Don't hurry.

Even at the start, it can take a long time to get into a nipple orgasm. Set aside some time to explore the sensation and figure out what makes you happy.

Get into the spirit.

It's important to be excited. If you're going on a date with or without a partner, think about music, lighting, and other cool things that can help set the mood.

Communicate

It's important to communicate with each other when having tantric sex. Keeping in touch can help ensure that everyone is having a good time. Describe how you like to be pinched, bit, or play with toys so that your partner knows what kind of sensations you like best.

Stimulate other parts of the body

While you're touching your nipples, try touching other parts of your body that are sexual, like your genitals. Focusing on many different things could help someone reach Orgasm or make the experience even more powerful.

Finally, touch the stomach and explore other areas around the breast, gently rubbing in and around your breast in clockwise motions before finally getting to the nipple. Rub it gently and smoothly with light touches, kisses, and little bites.

e.   Tongue and eyes

tongue and eyes are two powerful tools to use when you seek pleasure and connection. Tantric sex is all about connecting to your partner. Nothing feels more naturally connecting than a long and neck kiss that keeps you fully awake. Using a tongue can be very gentle and lovely, and one can resist a good kisser. So learn to kiss your partner very well, licking them up just to show how much they mean to you

Eyes contact is an impressive feature of tantric sex. It is so fundamental that it can determine the result achieved. Several tantra positions like yab yum or lotus allow you to lock eyes with your partner for a long time. Passing messages, establishing trust, and connecting you deeper than you can imagine.

f.   Glans

The glans refers to the tip of penis where ejaculation and semen is released. This part is very sensitive to men and can trigger the right energy from woman. When massage your partner, pay attention to rubbing and massaging the glans. This allows you to feel a special level of satisfaction. However, since this is tantra, you can still enjoy more minutes together without the fear of losing erection.

Chapter 8

Mastering love and overcoming emotions

Love is never a one-time feeling. It is a connection, commitment, and ability to stay focused - that is the art of mastering love.

We often think love is about seeing someone for the first time, being with them for weeks, and finding out that you just want to be around them. Yes, that is a feeling that can lead to something great if properly used.

However, we see relationships breaking up, marriages collapsing, and people who were once so intimate divorcing and swearing never to do a thing together again. This rampant development makes us doubt the existing belief about love and its origin.

Can it ever be true that love stops at finding comfort in someone?

Perhaps, a yes or no answer is impossible since finding comfort in another can be the greatest giver of joy. How a total stranger turns into a partner and someone, you can trust with your body and how a friend moves from being casual to someone you want to spend the rest of your life with. These are not misery but questions that can be answered when we take some time to look inward and realize just how much we've compromised, how much we've given, and how much time we have to say sorry for things that weren't so wrong to us. Suppose, at some point in life, you find yourself somewhere around here with someone who reciprocates with equal energy. In that case, it may be that you subconsciously discovered a life hack to bliss and happiness.

Whoever tells you to let go of love because it hurts, never do it the right way. Like every other thing in life, we need to master love and how to use our emotions the right way. Only then can we achieve the beauty, intimacy, and peace we seek.

Here are a few things to keep in mind as your progress through the journey

- **Start with a lot of self-love**

You cannot possibly express love and affection if you do not love yourself, so there is a need to fill every part of your life with enough love and light. Loving yourself transcends the act of having a lovely hang out or a weekend at the spa.

Self-love is accepting who you are, understanding who you are, and trusting the process when it does not seem too clear.

You will need to do all of these before you start a relationship to know when someone does not love you the way you deserve to be loved.

Lack of self-love will also affect your ability to love genuinely. Finding peace within is connected to finding peace with another person. It is ok to be hurt, broken, or trying to put the piece together, but at every point, never forget to love yourself.

- **Get the required clarity about love and want**

Love alone does not give satisfaction, and even where it does, it may not last. The body gets tired, and sometimes, the heart wants something else. But how do you wake up someone and discover you no longer feel the same?

While we can rule out the chance of falling out of love completely, having someone who checks some of your search lists may be a great way to keep your relationship together, find your right path, and take time to understand what they truly mean to you in the face of a hot argument of significant differences. Hence, it is important to be clear on love and the things you want.

Do this by setting up a list and never letting a person go if they do not meet all your requirements. Examine if you find them attractive and never fall in love just because there is a need to reciprocate the feeling they showed. Be clear with your wants and be confident about finding the right person.

- **Understand you can attract love**

Settling for less because you think it is impossible to find the right person is a no-no, and you do not want to do that to yourself. There is a need to understand that whoever is right for you will find their way toward you. So keep your list stable and your mind free till you find the best person.

The risk of settling is that the love never lasts even when the other person loves you just the same for a year. You will put yourself in a situation that may break your heart repeatedly. Not because you have a terrible partner but because you cannot reciprocate a sincere feeling. So do not take it from the start, and if you have, it is time to correct that.

- **Express love confidently**

Never hide your feelings; your partner deserves to know how much you love them. While we often keep the words and expect the other person to guess that we do, we are losing out on moments to create the greatest bond and memories that can affect our love.

Loving carefree when you have a lot to do and learning to express your love without shame or fear is an assurance of feeling, something you do to remind yourself of just how much someone means to you, and something you do to tell them that they mean a lot you.

It is not ok to get so lost in your feelings that you can no longer express them. If you like someone, tell them you. Take the bold step and never let your loved ones feel unloved.

- **Learn to resolve conflict**

Love may exist anywhere, but a healthy relationship does not. It takes the understanding of two people who are genuinely in love and care about each other to build a healthy relationship.

Incessant arguments are not healthy for a relationship, and expectedly, it is impossible to find two people who quarrel a lot in a healthy relationship. Don't get it wrong, it is possible to love someone and quarrel with them every day; however, that is not a healthy relationship.

Some of us think the next thing after a fight is never talking to our partner again. So when a little misunderstanding occurs, you assume the other person no longer wants to do anything with you.

When a conflict can be resolved, do not let it break the good thing you have going on. Develop a conflict-resolving mechanism where a party is not too big to apologize when they are wrong. Communicate differences and ensure that you do not hide from saying things that hurt you.

Learn to fight for yourself when you are hurt and never put your self-esteem in the way of keeping a relationship. Again, if it is a resolvable conflict, then resolve it.

- **Never let your ego win**

If there is one rule that works for a healthy relationship, it is never letting your ego take the best part of you.

We all make the mistake of letting the right person leave because we are angry at the moment, and it all seems like we do not care about what will happen. Several relationships no longer exist because the ego wins. If you can get to a point where your ego does not stop you from explaining yourself, you are near maintaining a healthy relationship.

Often we forget that a great partner is worth more than our ego. We let go of people who mean the world to us, hoping they will stay forever. However, we can be happier by understanding that ego is an enemy of stable, healthy relationships.

How do you build a better relationship?

Instead of focusing on being the best person or the right person for your partner, work on developing the right and strongest connection with them, for there is love in bonding.

Find time to bond and spend amazing moments together. Doing this will not need to try to be the best person because if you connect to someone deeply and find out that they are connected to you the same way, there can be no better person.

Building a connection is also a good solution to ego problems. Find things that make you connect to your partner deeper. You naturally prioritize their happiness over your ego when this happens, and it becomes hard to let them go.

Overcoming emotions

Emotion is a strong feeling or rush that gets us to something. Everything we feel is emotion, and they all have a significant impact on our life. The ability to feel and express emotion is a great feature we all possess. In some cases, it is what makes us human.

Tantric sex is a relationship is an emotion builder. A tool that can help develop great passion between two people. However, as much as we all want a relationship to last because they are so beautiful, we, once in a while, fall for people who do not intend to stay forever. Where you have developed emotions through activities like tantra, it may become hard to control or overcome such emotion, which may become detrimental even though it is a good emotion.

Being too happy may cause problems if you do not know how to control them, and being sad may be wrecking if you do not learn how to overcome them.

Overcoming emotion can be very hard since it is like a superior drive that controls how we act and react to situations. This is why a lot of self-restraining goes into controlling your emotions, and people who can do this tend to have the ability to control their lives.

Even if you do not possess superior self-restraining ability, it is possible to learn how to overcome emotions.

▪ Understand the impact of your emotion

When there is a need to overcome an emotion, you need to stop doing something you find irresistible. When it is stopping how you feel about someone, it is essentially moving on from someone you care about or find irreplaceable, so it can be hard

Do not blame yourself for your emotions, it is perfectly ok to get overwhelmed with your feelings, and absolutely nothing is wrong with that. However, it is important to understand the impact of your emotion.

When you are not getting the reciprocity you deserve, emotion can become a hard tool causing you a lot of pain. Take time to walk through it and keep the impact in mind.

▪ Identify and accept your emotions

Identify what you are feeling and learn to accept it. These are two connected steps that can flow naturally if you let them. Understanding why you are angry to ensure that you do not mix things up and attend to the necessary things will help you overcome emotion.

So take some moment to examine the situation, check with yourself, and find the reason behind this overwhelming emotion.

Calming the mind and understanding that you are not at fault is a good way to accept your feelings and take proper control.

First, you must find it in your mind to validate your feelings and give yourself some credit for having so much emotion and love to share because even if it does not look it, emotions make you an awesome person, and that is amazing.

Now, find comfort in your emotions, accept them and let them flow without reacting harshly to yourself.

- **Aim for regulation**

When the person you spend time loving is not reciprocating, it is obvious, but it can be hard to believe. At first, you may start by blaming yourself; however, you need to understand that the only thing you can control is your emotion and not how others feel about you.

At this point, it gets hard, but you must find a way to regulate your emotion. Learn to let go when people want to leave, and do not stop believing that you can attract the right person that will love you the right way.

Important tips when trying to overcome emotion

- **Exercise**

Exercising is a good way to free your mind, so try it when you cannot control how you feel. For the moment, it will effectively calm you down and let you focus on your fitness goal. This way, you can forget about what happened a moment ago and move on to the next thing.

If this affects you for long, I recommend starting a long-term fitness goal and ensuring that jugging or hitting the gym is the first thing you do every day. This puts you in a good mood by releasing feel-good hormones. Hence, you can get through each day feeling comfortable.

- **Practice mindfulness**

Taking some minutes off to practice mindfulness every day is a good way to stay in control. One benefit of this meditating process is that it allows you to focus on one thing for a long time. So when you put effort into overcoming your emotion, mindfulness can equip you with the right mind to get it done.

Chapter 9

Tantric Sex Positions

Several sex positions can help to tantra. These positions have the inherent ability to allow you to communicate and feel your partner better. You will realize you are in a better position even after the sex as you do this.

Love and relationship revolve around spending quality time together and having a strong emotional and sexual connection that makes you feel your partner is irreplaceable. Achieving this is possible, and you enjoy your love life better than anyone when you pay attention to your body and mind together.

Sex will not be a key to your relationship sustenance. Still, through it, you will learn to grow with each, appreciate each other's company and find genuine interest in things that make you happy together.

You will also find alignment in sexual preferences. Even when you like some positions better, understanding that your partner's needs matter just like yours, will you give a mind ready to compromise? This will eventually reflect on other parts of your life.

It is also important to understand that some sexual positions may not suit your partner, and some may be considered unnecessary and stressful. While tantric sex is for exploration, doing things that are more fun for both parties should be your priority. This is where the minds can open and intertwine on a similar level.

Tantric sex positions are effective for everyone, and you just have to select the ones that work well for you. The age, gender, and body of your partner should be considered as you do not want to suggest positions that are not suitable for them

Setting the mood for the best tantric sex experience

For tantric sex, the mood is everything. Since this will be a long activity that helps you bond beautifully with your partner, there is a need to properly plan how you want the evening to go. This is enough to get your partner in the ready mood.

Spicing things up in a relationship is not a one-person duty; however, if you are one to notice the spark fading off, it is your duty to take charge of the situation and bring your partner back to track.

We must understand that love and life can get wary with times. This is not a lack of love but a sign that your partner needs you now. If you are in this kind of situation, doing your best is the only solution to find out what is truly going on. Your partner will appreciate you for genuinely bringing them back into memories. While this does not mean you were never together, it ignites the feelings again. Everything starts to work perfectly fine again.

The truth is, we all get tired of things. While your relationship may not be a problem, your partner may be dealing with different phases of life that get them bothered and lost in their own beliefs. Let them know how much you want to be there for them by taking their mind off all the hassle and making them feel uniquely loved. You will be surprised at how much light and love you carry, and when you realize how this matters, you will not help but appreciate yourself for not giving up on them easily.

This does not mean you must beg for love, know the right person who loves you, and learn to understand that everything around us controls our mood and how we interact with important people.

Trying for your love life is one of the best decisions you will make. Giving up when there is still a chance of redeeming your relationship only sets you up for another relationship tussle. Hence, we must understand the clear line between giving up and letting go and knowing when they apply to our situations.

1. Tanta During Oral Sex

First and foremost, remember to establish eye contact. Do not be concerned if the position doesn't look "porny." Looking lovingly at your spouse when you fall upon him is possible, and he can do the same for you. Using your hands during sex is a terrific way to combine your full body in the experience.

Gently breathe on and around your partner's genitals before applying pressure with your mouth to his genitals. Regardless of whether your hands or mouth are making contact with your partner's body, you can still picture the transference of sexual energy between you.

Finally, remember not to judge yourself when performing or receiving oral sex. This will help you stay mindful.

2. Hands-on hearts circuit

After staring into each other's eyes, this one is generally a good fit. Bring your hands to your own heart and breathe up into your heart while facing each other with a loving stare. Put your right hand on your partner's chest (with their permission) as you feel the love rising in your heart for them. They can do the same for you.

Slow, deep, nourishing breaths are the key to synchronizing your breathing. Receive air and love into your own heart while exhaling and sending it down your right arm to your partner's heart, forming a circuit of love and energy between you. Do this for roughly ten breaths at a time.

3. Spooning

A significant feature of tantric sex is performing intimate meditation with a partner, which is made possible by spooning. Both partners should be lying on their side, facing in the same direction, with the length of their bodies touching each other. Their chakras — seven points on the body that are believed to be energy centers, such as the heart, navel, and "third eye" location on the forehead — would align with one another. Using deep inhalations and exhalations simultaneously, they can harmonize their breath while also focusing on either transmitting or receiving energy.

4. The Sidewinder

This posture, which is similar to the spooning position but with both partners looking in the same direction, results in a great deal of kissing and eye contact. It's simple to get into this position: turn the missionary posture on its side, and you're done. Depending on your comfort level, one leg may remain under the man's legs, or both legs may be resting together over his legs. Concentrate on matching your breathing and getting more rhythm with your partner's emotions.

Below are some of the positions to try

1. The Goddess Pose

Goddess pose is a tantric sex position that focuses on keeping eye contact. Remember that eye gazing is an important way to engage in tantra. This feature is also what makes the goddess pose great. An ecstatic flow and constant breathing keep you at the moment. Both parties will enjoy each other the most, and the moment will be filled with connection arising from constant eye contact.

The inserting partner (the guy) lies comfortably on his back, allowing the woman to squat over his penis and achieve penetration. It is a cowgirl position, and the essence is that you get to look at each other right in the face allowing vulnerabilities to flow away and confidence begins to form.

2. Yab Yum

The yab yum position is the frequently recommended because it keeps you glued to each other. In a yab yum position, you will be sitting close to each other so much that the receptive party is on the penetrating party's lap, and you can look into each other eyes and breathe along. This is one of the most romantic moments in tantra, and the impact can be stronger if you let it. There is eye contact, communication, and conscious breathing. Keep the intimacy and embrace alive by affirming your feelings for one another and synchronizing breathing.

The penetrating partner will sit with his leg crossed. The receptive partner will sit on the penetrating partner's leg with her leg straddled. This creates enough space for the penetration of the penis and keeps the parties close to each other. There is also nipples rubbing the other party's both and increasing the level of pleasure derived.

Maintain this position for as long as possible without hesitating to rock each other wildly and back and forth.

3. The swing

While this position keeps the rider in control, it is just as satisfying for the penetrating partner. Two results are achieved simultaneously, so this pose is a great option. If you are a woman or with a woman who is trying to do away with shyness during sex, this is a good position to try. The swing keeps the riding partner in control and allows emotions to flow. There is also clitoris stimulation assisting the riding partner in identifying her own sexual desire.

Let the penetrating partner lays comfortably on their back with a range to lower or lift the pelvis. Then the receptive partner will ride the other partner taking control of the moment. The effect is achieving a swinging position that allows the parties to move gently, stimulating sexual satisfaction in both of them

4. Open pincer

Open pincer is another great sex position with tantric property. For starting, it allows you to participate in more sexual activities than the regular penis and vagina penetration. It is great for anal sex to create space in the vulva for the deeper vagina penetration.

Aside from that, it is not like simple casual sex because it allows you to focus on things that help build rapport. You can easily maintain eye contact and share breathing with your partner.

The receptive partner lays down lying under a pillow placed right under their hips (can be done without a pillow). The penetrating partner holds the leg of the receptive partner in their hands while remaining on their knees, creating a comfortable chance for penetration.

The receptive partner lays down with their legs in the penetrative partner's hands. The penetrative partner is on their knees and directs themselves inside the receiving partner.

5. Third eye bliss

Third eye bliss is like the missionary way, but it gives room for more intimacy. You can look into each other's eyes and follow slow and steady emotion building and intimacy. This allows you to feel the sexual energy within your body.

6. Tiger pose

This position allows you to relax your body and feel the moment. This does not mean that the sexual satisfaction is reduced; you can go slow and thrust deeper.

Similar to the spooning position, just that there is more space between the partners. Lie down next to your partner to form this position. Both parties should be on their sides.

7. Serpent embrace

Serpent embrace allows you to connect deeply with your spouse, and it comes with an added benefit, you can touch and massage each other hip.

The receptive partner will lay on their stomach with legs spread slightly apart by placing their arms by the side. Putting a pillow at their back is a good option here. Then, the insertive partner will lay on top of their partner, resting their forearms on the bed to prop themselves up slightly.

To enjoy the most intense, connected, and intimate orgasms of your life, you're about to master tantric sex. Here are several sex positions that ensure that tantra deepens your relationship with your lover by showing you the finest positions.

8. The Hot seat:

Your partner kneels, and you also kneel so that your bodies touch as much as possible. During this time, your legs will be in his way. He can reach between your legs and rub your clit, or wrap his arms around your hips or waist. You can move your hips up and down or in a circle. Your hips will move the way you want them to move. Feel free to take a break if this work is too much for you.

It's time to change things up. Sit on his lap with your knees bent. So, like a lap dance, he'll be able to see your butt move backward, which will let you grind it against him. It might be fun to try this backseat driver position on a couch.

9. The Butterfly

You need flat and low furniture, like a table or a bed, to do this tantric sex. Lie down on the ground. He will hold you by the butt to lift your hips as he stands. This is the best way to rest your ankles on his shoulders. When you're in the butterfly position, your back will leave the table. You can use your arms to keep your body in place. An extra pillow under your back or hips can help.

Your partner will feel like their penis is bigger if you close your legs and hold them straight up.

10. The Padlock

The first step to obtaining the padlock is to lean on the edge of the counter, a piece of furniture, or an appliance while facing your partner and attempting to unlock it. Your lover takes a step between your legs, and you wrap your arms around him at the waist. Use your arms to provide yourself more leverage and better view your partner's body. This also gives him access to your clitoral region!

11. Kali on the ball pose

Kali is another Hindu deity, and the ball serves as her partner in this game (no pun intended). A squat is performed by one person holding their partner's legs while the other holds their partner's chest to maintain balance. In this position, one partner sits on the floor while the other squats over their lap with their back to their chest. Afterward, both should move softly back and forth between the two positions.

12. The Double Decker

A woman reclining on top of a guy while facing away is considered one of the most effective sex positions for mutual fulfillment and connection. Put yourself in the reverse cowgirl position and lean back against his chest to get things started. Sliding motion can be created by pressing your feet against the bed and creating control over the situation. Please take pleasure in his warm breathing on your neck and pay attention to his instructions.

This position is excellent if you have difficulty coming since it allows you to maintain complete control—and it is also the ideal position to incorporate a tantra sex toy.

13. The Lotus

A great way to increase intimacy and sexual satisfaction in your yoga practice is to adopt the lotus position, also known as the yab yum pose.

The penetrating partner sits cross-legged on the floor or in bed with their legs crossed. You both rock back and forth while the receiver straddles your lover, wrapping their legs around their partner's waist and maintaining eye contact.

In addition, the partner on top can lean backward to receive greater g-spot stimulation.

14. The Lap dance

It is possible to adapt the Edge of Heaven tantra position to any chair or stable surface in your home if you do not have a proper bed or couch for this position.

The receiving partner crosses their legs over their partner's shoulders, leans back, and clutches their lover's thighs for support. The giving partner does the same.

Consider using a chair with a high back so that the penetrating partner can rest and take in the view while sitting in the chair.

15. The delight

This position, sometimes called a tantric missionary, is simple and easy to do, but it allows for deep intimacy between partners even if they don't touch each other. The receptive partner should sit on the edge of the bed, and the penetrating partner should stand in front of them. Legs are wrapped around each other's bodies by the seated partner, who may have to kneel. They then lie back and rest.

When one person stands, they can stay upright or lean forward on their hands. Both partners can see each other's faces and stroke their bodies from this position, encouraging them to pay attention. When you stay in this position for a while before you try to get in, the connection will be very strong when and if you do. Like any tantric sex practice, the connection brings it up to a level where one is in touch with the Universe through one's partner and the world.

16. Reverse seated

It would help if you had the guy kneeling next to the person you're with. She should be facing him with her back to him and his legs on the ground. If you're not a guy or a girl, try to find a version of this position that works for both of you. If you're not a yoga person, you can still do this one. But if you want to get into someone, it's best to have the person who wants to get in behind you.

Do nothing now. Just enjoy the feeling of skin on skin and seeing each other's bodies, and don't worry about what you look like.

It's possible to get into this position when you're ready. As long as the person in front doesn't move, that's all you need to do. The person in the back should embrace the person in front to help them keep their weight down. A lot of skin contact, fingertip tracing, and neck nuzzling can happen in this position. You may have to try different moves to find one that works for both of you, but it's worth it.

17. Scissors

The name says everything. As you all lay down, legs intertwined and sex parts in contact with each other, your heads were at different ends. Each of you acts as a conduit for the energy that moves through the Universe when you are together but spread out. This one helps you both stay in balance while also allowing you to connect. Or, it might just make you feel great. Both ways are good.

This is a great place for lovers who like to play foot games. In this position, one partner's leg will be on top, crossing over the crease of their partner's groin. The partner on the bottom can easily reach it for stroking. The feet can be massaged or kissed, and they can also be brushed. The toes are near the mouth. In the beginning, you can start grinding each other without letting go of the legs or feet to make each other feel more excited. Anyone who has ever had sex while someone is sucking on their toes should put it on their bucket list.

18. The merger

The name sounds like a business job, but this is a sex job that allows for eye contact, conversation, and even caressing. It also lets each person control the depth and speed of penetration, so you can both drive simultaneously.

People who want to get to know each other sit on top of each other, straddling each other and facing each other. Similar to the Yab-Yum pose, but the legs are not crossed. Each person then leans back, putting their weight on their hands. If you bend your legs at this point, it may be more comfortable for you to do so.

Make gentle finger strokes over each other's bodies, backs, or faces as long as you want in this pose. Or you could just look at each other and breathe together. In this case, go as slowly as you can. That's what this pose is all about. Experiment with how far or low you can go to see how far you can go. Slowly speed up and match your thrusts so that you both flow into each other. As your lover cries, pay attention to what they say. Could you take a deep breath and smell them? It is possible to see stars.

19. Sky dancing

In the Buddhist tradition, "Sky Dancers" were passionate people who vigorously pursued enlightenment. You and your love collaborate on your shared enlightenment, joining your bodies and blending your consciousness in this position. It's also a wonderful position for unleashing a woman's sensual drive, as it allows her to be in control while her lover lies passively beneath her, to be used in service of her joy.

This looks like your traditional woman on top position. When she leans back, she affords her partner a view of her Yoni (tantra word for the female sex organ). She can show her love how she wishes to be pleasured. She can lean forward to kiss their lips or pour hot breathy whispers into their ear. She can take them into her body when she wants to, thrusting and undulating at her own ideal pace until passion takes her to the breaking point. This is the sky dance.

20. The Great Bee

Putting someone in the Great Bee position means the penetrating partner lies down on their back, and the receiving partner rides them. You can tell it's based on Cowgirl, but with one big difference. The top partner pulls their legs toward their chest as if they were doing a deep squat like they are. They can put their arms on their partner's chest to help them feel safe and strong.

The word "thrusting" usually refers to a movement that goes in and out, but this position focuses on experiencing intercourse differently. Her partner should make circles or move back and forth or tilt to one side. Queen says this is the best way for them to get in. If you want some really deep thrusting, but not very quickly, this is where.

21. The golden retriever

We are not criticizing Doggy-style, although it can sometimes feel like it is right for tantric moment. Ensure that this posture is tantric-friendly. The root chakra, an erogenous region that gives us a sense of safety and belonging, is best opened in this position.

Begin with the receiving partner on all fours and the penetrating partner behind them in a conventional doggie style. Have the penetrator wrap their body over their partners instead of clutching at the receiver's hips. The receiver can arch their back to trigger the heart's energy center. Skin-to-skin contact can now be more easily achieved.

22. Sensual fork

Because it's intimate, sensual, and helps you get very close to your partner, the Sensual Fork is one of the best tantric sex positions. In this position, almost every part of your body will be touched, which you want to happen.

One leg is bent a little over the knee of the partner on the bottom. This is how the top partner moves behind them. They slide their leg between the bottom partner's legs as they penetrate. You both can either lay down or put a pillow under your side to help you stay upright to see each other's faces better.

Try to keep your eyes locked on your partner, share kisses as you have sex, and breathe deeply to improve the experience.

23. The spread eagle

There are several cool ways to stimulate your partner in the Spread-Eagle position. However, it's still very intimate, so it's a good choice for tantric sex.

During penetration, the bottom partner lays on their back on the bed or other surface with their legs up and spread wide. The top partner then moves to the end of the bed or surface.

When two people are having intercourse, the top person keeps the lower legs of their partner up by their ankles, so they can move the legs around to try out different angles if they need to during the intercourse.

The Spread Eagle is great for getting into your vagina and inner genitals. Another good thing about this tool is that both partners can use it to stimulate the clitoral area. It's also good for deep penetration angles that will hit all the right places.

During this sex position, it's also easy to keep eye contact and share breath. It's also a very relaxing and comfortable position to be in.

24. The Perch Pose

Perch is another sitting tantric sex position that is just as fun as others. One added advantage is that it allows the penetrating partner to caress the body of the receiving partner, paving the way for a more romantic and meaningful moment.

How to do this:

The penetrating partner sits on a stool or chair while the receiving partner sits on his lap facing the other direction. The receiving partner may be required to lean to the front a little for penetration. After that, the receiving partner can lean backward and control the penetration with their leg. More thrusting is enhanced as the receiving partner relies on their legs for strength.

25. The Balancing Act

The balancing Act is a tantra position that requires some flexibility. Hence it is recommended only when you can move out being extremely comfortable during sex. The best part is that it is just as effective as others because it allows each party to focus on their energy, enjoy the moment and spend that exploring fancier sex experiences.

How to do this:

The penetrating partner will lie on his back with his legs open apart. The receiving partner will sit down on his thighs, facing the other direction. The receiving partner will further curl her body in a ball-like position, and the man will support her for balance.

Since this position is a little difficult to maintain, you can enjoy an easy ride and new sex style for a few minutes and proceed to the other ones. You can also stop here. It all depends on what works and makes you feel the other person more.

26. The Curled Angel Pose

This is an easy tantra position that enhances closeness in a relationship. As you stay close to each other during sex, you are bound to feel each other's body and breathing. Also, you can enjoy this position for a long time, making it an ideal sex position for developing long affection.

How to do this:

Doing this is quite easy. The receiving partner will curl their body, and the penetrating partner will curl into them from the back, allowing easy penetration. Once this is done, you can enjoy a smooth sex time that does not stop you from deep thrusting and enjoying wilder passion. The penetrating partner can also fondle the receiving partner's breast or the nipple.

27. The Bridge Pose

The bridge is a recommendable sex position if you like to spice things up and take your sex life to another level. By focusing on your energy and the need for balance, you aid each other and understand how much satisfaction is derived from the activities. Keep the minutes low to avoid stressing yourself, and do not try the pose if you find it too complex.

How to do this:

The penetrating partner will bend backward, resting his weight on his feet and hand. The receiving partner will then straddle them and enhance penetration. The receiving partner uses their feet to enhance thrusting and can even lift off their weight from the penetrating partner by supporting themselves with their feet.

28. The Kneel Pose

For tantric sex, even the easiest sex pose is effective and fun. The kneeling pose is ideal for almost everything that keeps your bond stronger. You can practice maintaining eye contact, communicating, and breathing more during sex.

How to do this:

Both the receiving and the penetrating partner will face each other in a kneeling position. The receiving partner then places their legs on the other side of the penetrating partner's leg, allowing easy penetration. This position is easy to maintain and can give you a lovely experience without any discomfort.

29. Splitting Bamboo Pose

Another fantastic position for the tantric moment is the splitting bamboo pose. This position is good for those trying to practice eye contact. As you get lost in the ecstasy, you can also see each other; know how much the other person can make you feel good. However, the position requires some flexibility and should only be practiced by those that can do that.

How to do this

The receiving partner will lie on their back with one leg hanging in the air, and the other stretched out flat. The penetrating partner then comes in between their thighs and penetrates while holding on to the elevated leg in the air. The receiving partner can then bring their leg down on the penetrating partner's leg.

30. The Clip Pose

Another tantra position to try is the clip pose. Representing a more fantastic sex experience, the clip will get you lost in each other bodies paving the way for more thoughtful yet sexually satisfying moments. The position also enhances eye gazing allowing partners to establish trust and vulnerability.

How to do this:

The penetrating partner lies on their back with their legs outstretched and closed. The receiving partner will then sit on the penetrating partner inserting the penis in her vagina as she does. The receiving partner will then lean back and support herself on her arms a little, enabling herself to grind the penetrating partner smoothly.

31. The Close-Up Pose

This position is more of an intentional sex position. It is simple to do and yet remains meaningful for the two parties. It also allows easy penetrating and deep thrusting; hence, it helps keep the moment alive with good sex.

How to do this:

The receiving partner lies on their side, and the penetrating partner will do the same. With their legs widely opened, the receiving partner will then pushes their hips into the penetrating partner and wrap their legs around the penetrating partner for easy penetration.

32. The Hero Pose

If wild passion is your desire, this medium-rated sex position is one of the best ways to enjoy each other's bodies and understand that there is more exploration to do with time.

How to do this:

The pose begins with the receiving partner lying on their back with their knees pulled up to their chest. They then raise their feet up to face the ceiling. The penetrating partner will then kneel, facing them and thrusting in the receiving partner. The penetrating partner should support the receiving partner by helping them hold their legs, so they do not get tired easily.

33. The Dolphin Pose

The Dolphin tantra pose is a sex position that allows both eyes gazing and communicate. You understand how you feel by seeing each other, and you even say it out. it is advisable to practice communication during tantra to elevate each other's mood and end the with a good feeling and reaffirmation of love.

How to do this:

The receiving partner will lie on the bed and slightly lift their waist up. They then rest their weight on their head and shoulder while the penetrating partner's knee faces them and penetrates. More support is needed so the penetrating partner can support the receiving partner with their pelvis and hand.

34. The Frog Pose

The frog pose is something to try out for more fun and overwhelming sex experience

How do this:

The penetrating partner will sit at the edge of the bed around the corner, placing his feet comfortably on the floor. The receiving partner will then crouch on the penetrating partner's lap, making the frog pose. The receiving partner is supported by the penetrating partner's thighs as they press on for a deeper thrust.

35. The Fan Pose

The fan pose is a good sex position for easy penetration. Though it may be a little uncomfortable, it can be enjoyed for some time before changing to an easy one.

How to do this:

The position begins with the receiving partner bending their knees and resting them on the edge of a stool or chair. The receiving partner will also keep their hand on the back of that stool or chair for strength and the penetrating partner will penetrate them from the back.

36. The Amazon Pose

Amazon allows the receiving partner to take control, paving the way for more sexual pleasure that does not get the penetrating partner to do anything other than sit down and enjoy the moment. It is effective for bonding between partners.

How to do this:

The penetrating partner will sit on a stool or chair, and the receiving partner will sit gently on him with the two parties facing each other. The penetrating partner will then penetrate the receiving partner, and both of them can practice eye gazing as they moan in ecstasy.

37. The Crossed Keys Pose

The penetrating partner has some work to do during this sex position. I recommend saving it as the last piece as there is a lot to enjoy, and you can get tired afterward and cuddle each other for long. It is also suitable for eye gazing, making it an ideal sex position when you are ready to get lost in each other body and appreciate the love within.

How to do this:

The receiving partner lies near the edge of the bed, keeping her legs up and crossed at the knee. The penetrating partner then stands facing her and penetrates her. The penetrating partner has the duty of holding her leg up, crossing and uncrossing them as he thrusts deeper into the receiving partner.

38. The Snail Pose

Another great position to enjoy with your partner is the snail pose. One good thing about this position is that it is recommended for most people and allows you to grow rapport with your partner through eye gazing.

How to do this:

The receiving partner will lie on their back and bring their knees to the chest to get this position. The penetrating partner will then kneel in the front of the receiving partner allowing the receiving partner to put their legs over his shoulder. This allows easy penetration, and the penetrating partner can maintain balance by their hands on the side of the receiving partner.

39. The Proposal Pose

Another sex position to enjoy while facing each other. This is not a simple eye contact pose but allows you to look deep into your partner's eye and see what you are making them feel. It can eliminate vulnerability, establish trust, and create a more impactful sexual life that keeps your daily life more romantic. It is also a very easy pose to maintain; anyone can try it.

How to do this:

Both partners will start the position by kneeling down while facing one another. The penetrating partner will mimic the regular proposing pose by putting their left foot on the ground. The receiving partner replicates this by putting their right foot on the floor and moving closer to the penetrating partner. The penetrating partner then thrusts into the receiving partner, and the fun kicks in.

40. The Galley Pose

Finally, the galley pose is the last on our list. It is a great sex position that allows both parties to have a wonderful sex experience. If you love to shift a little from your comfort zone and try something new, put it on your list.

How to do this:

The penetrating partner will sit with their legs outstretched while weighing on one arm. The other handle should be kept free to fondle and caress their partner's body. The receiving partner sits on top of the penetrating partner for penetration. Once there is penetration, the receiving partner can lean back to the front while getting support from their arms. The receiving partner enhances penetration and movement while the penetrating partner fondles the breast, plays with the nipples, or just caresses the receiving partner's body.

What you should know

Tantric Solo Sex

Most information about tantric sex is based on the assumption that you'll require a partner, but this doesn't rule out the possibility of enjoying tantric sex alone or as part of a couple. While masturbating, you can use components of tantra to your advantage. This could signify one of the following:

• Concentrating on taking slow, deep breaths with extended exhales

• Visualize sensual energy coursing through your entire body and mind.

• Allowing lots of time for "foreplay" activities is important.

• Getting rid of clutter and making time and place only for masturbation are two important steps.

• Getting to know your entire body

• Allowing negative or judgmental ideas to pass by without being attached to them

• Accepting and respecting your body's sexual requirements and preferences

Conclusion

Love can be found anywhere and everywhere, and when the moment is right between two people who genuinely care for each other, it can be redeemed. Many sex positions and insightful ideas on how to keep your love life effective are shared in this book; however, you are a major determinant of how well this works for you.

Change starts from within; hence, making up your mind to enjoy more life and emotion-filled sex is one way to prepare your mind for worthwhile intercourse.

There is a lot to do, but it is more important to look within and see if you are ready for this. Your love life won't be all rosy, and as you grow, your partner will need you to take charge in situations where they do not find enough spark within themselves. Do not fail them. Take your time to understand what they are going through. Do not condemn them but show them that your love is enough to keep their mind from wandering around. Let them find peace within you, and you will be surprised how well they will reciprocate that.

We will not always find the right people in the right places. Also, relationships will be tested several times with life hurdles, changes, and growth. How much longer you hold on to each other and how well you understand that trusting this person is not wrong will go a long mile to determine how well you enjoy each other's presence.

If there is ever a thing to be for someone you love, it is being the light that lets them see all the love and emotions you carry. Wait for them to reciprocate, and your world can become as colorful as you want it.

Printed in Great Britain
by Amazon

85438195R00050